A New True Book

NATIVE AMERICANS

By Jay Miller

CP CHILDRENS PRESS®
CHICAGO

Books and movies made the Indians famous for their love of horses and daring deeds. But not all Native Americans wore feathers or rode horses.

PHOTO CREDITS

Arizona Historical Society Library — 22 (left)

© Reinhard Brucker — 25, 30 (top and bottom right); Field Museum, Chicago, 40 (top and bottom right)

© Michael Crummett — 45 (left)

© John Elk III — 26 (right), 28, 32

© Virginia R. Grimes — 36, 39

H. Armstrong Roberts — 7 (center), 27 (right)

Historical Pictures/Stock Montage, Inc. — 24, 27 (left)

Minnesota Historical Society — 14

Nawrocki Stock Photo — © W. S. Nawrocki — 43

North Wind Picture Archives — 17

© North Wind Pictures — Maine State Museum, 11 (right)

Odyssey/Frerck/Chicago — © E. S. Curtis, 8, 20 (right), 30 (left), 31 (left)

Archives & Manuscripts Division of the Oklahoma Historical Society — #20462.2.7 Pub. Lithograph by F. W. Greenough, Philadelphia, PA, 1836, 7 (left)

Photri — © Burciaga, 5 (right); © Lani, 26 (left)

R/C Photo Agency — © Richard Capps, 38; © Jane Kriete, 40 (left)

© Branson Reynolds — 13, 15 (right)

© James P. Rowan — Milwaukee County Museum, 35

Courtesy of the Royal Ontario Museum, Toronto, Canada — 37

© John Running — 6, 12 (right), 29, 31 (right)

© Smithsonian Institution — Charles M. Bell, 1880, 7 (right)

Tom Stack & Associates — © Robert Winslow, 2

State Historical Society of Wisconsin — 15 (left) Neg. No. (x3) 15462

Tony Stone Images — © James Chimbidis, 22 (right)

SuperStock International, Inc. — 11 (left); © Karl Kummels, Cover, 20 (left), 45 (right); © Prim and Ray Manley, 5 (left); © White Cloud, Chief of the Ioways, by George Catlin, 19 (left)

Valan — © John Cancalosi, 12 (left)

Wyoming State Museum — 19 (right)

Cover: Two young girls, Navajo Tribal Fair, Window Rock, AZ

Library of Congress Cataloging-in-Publication Data

Miller, Jay, 1947–
    Native Americans / By Jay Miller.
       p.   cm.–(A New true book)
    Includes index.
    Summary: Describes the culture, leadership, and structure of various tribes of Native Americans.
    ISBN 0-516-01192-8
    1.   Indians of North America–Juvenile Literature.
[1.   Indians of North America.] I. Title. II. Series.
E77.4.M55   1993
973'.0497–dc20
                        93-3442
                        CIP
                        AC

TABLE OF CONTENTS

NATIVE AMERICANS

A native is someone who belongs to a particular place. Native Americans are people who belong to the Americas. They knew America better than anyone else because

A Navajo sand painting (left) shows the world of the spirits who cure diseases. Pueblo women (right) wear their best clothes and carry colorful water jars on their heads in a parade.

they had lived here for thousands of years.

Sometimes these natives are called Indians, but that is not their own name for themselves. When European explorers first

A native rock painting in Canyon de Chelly in Arizona shows Spaniards on horseback.

came to the Americas, they thought they were in India. They called the American natives "Indians," and the name stuck. Now, even Native Americans sometimes call themselves Indians.

But Native Americans

Payta-kootha, a Shawnee (left), a Seminole woman with a child (center), and Red Cloud, a Lakota Sioux leader (right)

did not have one name
that meant all of their
people. Every tribe–and
there were thousands of
tribes–had its own name.
The name of each tribe
meant they were the best
human beings there were.

7

A summer camp with a canoe and a reed-mat tent, built by the Skokomish (Twana) of Washington State

TRIBES

All over the Americas, people lived along rivers. People who lived along the same river shared the same land, language, customs, rituals, and beliefs. They formed a grouping called a tribe. Members of the same tribe shared an understanding of how things should be done correctly.

Every tribe thought it was different from its neighbors.

Tribal leaders traded and talked with each other. They shared food and special gifts from their own lands. In this way, shells from the ocean, copper from the Great Lakes, mica from the West, and obsidian from the Great Plains moved back and forth across North America.

A culture is a combination of ideas, actions, and habits. Babies learn their culture as they grow up in a certain place with certain people. Culture teaches people how to speak, act, pray, and live.

The peoples of the Americas had many cultures and languages. The biggest difference

A farming town (left) called Secotan, near the colony of Virginia in the 1660s. The painting at right shows a camp of hunters from thousands of years ago.

among the Native Americans was between those people who lived by farming and those who lived by hunting animals and gathering plants.

11

FARMERS AND CARETAKERS

Native American farmers were the first to grow many crops that are found all over the world today—beans, squash, potatoes, tomatoes, sunflowers, and many kinds of corn.

Native gardens included many crops that have spread around the world. At right, a Hopi man holds colorful ears of corn.

Pueblo men and women dance to thank the spirits for their crops.

Thousands of years ago, the ancestors of these farmers figured out how to plant these crops and to improve them every year. With a mixture of hard work and prayers, their crops grew.

Ojibwa man and woman gathering wild rice in Minnesota. The woman uses two sticks to beat the grains into the canoe.

The caretakers, who hunted animals and gathered plants, took good care of their environment. They took only what they needed to feed themselves. They always prayed to the spirits of the plants

Two Ojibwa men (above) hunt wearing
snowshoes. A Hopi man (right)
dresses to look like a deer
for a thanksgiving dance.

and animals to thank them
for the nourishing food.

In North America,
farmers lived mostly in the
east and south. Caretakers
lived in the west and north. **15**

HOMES

Many Native Americans liked to travel during the year. But every tribe had a special place where they spent the winter together.

The kind of houses that Native Americans lived in told a lot about how they lived with nature and with each other. People built their houses with whatever materials were nearby, but they did this in many clever ways. Did they use wood, stone, bone, or

skins? That depended on
where they lived.

The men usually did the
building, but not always
and everywhere.
Sometimes women built
and owned houses.

Native women make the framework for a bark-covered house at a family camp.

LEADERS

Men were the leaders in each tribe, but women also had a say in how things were done. Usually, there were four kinds of leaders—the chief, the captain, the doctor, and the priest. Men usually filled these positions, but sometimes a woman became a leader.

The chief, who watched out for everyone, was usually a kind man from a good family. He helped

White Cloud (left), a chief of the Ioways, and
Washakie (right), a leader from Wyoming

the people decide when
to harvest plants and
when to hold gatherings.

The captain was a
warrior, or soldier, who
defended the town and its
people. During a war, he
led attacks on enemies.

19

A Cherokee holy man (left) with his herbs and medicines. A Hopi man (right) who belongs to the Snake priesthood is dressed for a ritual.

The doctor fasted and prayed to contact the spirits who gave him medicines and the knowledge of how to cure the sick.

The priest led his

people in worship and

rituals. Every year, when the crops were ripe and the berries were ready to be picked, or the fish came up the river, the priest held a ceremony to give thanks to the spirits.

When a boy or girl was given a name or when someone died, the priest led the tribal rituals.

These jobs usually passed from father to son. If your father was a chief, you would grow up to become a chief, too.

Apache women (left) in the late 1800s, in front of a brush shelter, which protected them from the wind and sun. A modern Apache girl (right) goes through a ceremony to mark her coming of age as a woman.

Sometimes women were the doctors and priests when the rituals marked events in the life of a woman. The changes from girl to woman, woman to wife, and wife to mother were celebrated by the women.

FARMING TRIBES

Among most farmers, women worked the fields and gathered wild fruits and nuts. The men fished and hunted.

Families were related through the mothers. Fathers, who belonged to another family, loved their children but did not raise them. Children were raised by the mother's brothers because they were all descendants of the same grandmother.

An Iroquois town with longhouses covered with bark. The women are making pots, drying and roasting corn, and filling storage pits with food for the winter.

THE NORTHEAST

The farmers of the Northeast lived in large houses. Grandmothers, mothers, daughters, and their families lived together.

Tribes such as the Iroquois and Delaware lived in longhouses. These houses were made of bent saplings covered with bark slabs. Each family had its own space in the longhouse.

The inside of a longhouse, showing the bunks along the sides where the family sat and slept on mats of corn husks covered with skins

This temple of reeds and plaster (above) was built on top of a mound of earth.

THE SOUTHEAST

In the Southeast, the Creek and Cherokee lived in houses made of plaster and reeds. Their temples and the homes of their leaders were built on top of high earth mounds. The mounds were made by piling up dirt carried in baskets.

After the Spanish, French, and English came to the Southeast, many Creek and Cherokee were killed in wars. Some fled to the Florida Everglades. These refugees became the Seminole tribe.

A Seminole village in the Florida Everglades. Seminoles wore clothes made of tiny pieces of colorful cloth sewn together. The women used alligator skin to make other things.

Pueblo families still live in this three-story adobe
building at Taos, New Mexico. People have lived here
for hundreds of years.

THE SOUTHWEST

In the deserts of the
Southwest, the Pueblo
people built houses like
modern apartment
buildings. They were made
of wood, stone, and
adobe. Many families

28

shared the same building.

Although the Southwest gets little rain, the Pueblo people were able to grow crops. They dug ditches to bring water from streams to their fields. They also prayed for rain by dancing at ceremonies.

For centuries, Pueblo

Pueblo men and women in New Mexico dance to ask for rain for their crops.

A Pueblo woman (left) makes pottery using coiled clay strips. Every Pueblo group in New Mexico has its own way of making pottery. Acoma Pueblo pottery (top right) and Zuni Pueblo pottery (bottom right) are examples. Today, pottery is made for sale to tourists and collectors.

women have made beautiful painted pottery. Pueblo men wove cotton cloth long before the Europeans arrived.

A Blackfoot man and his horse (left) stand in front of a painted tipi. Though Native Americans now live in ordinary houses, tipis (right) might be set up in the yard for use during the warm summer months.

CARETAKER TRIBES

In the West and North, people moved often. They hunted, fished, and gathered plants, seeds, roots, and berries. They lived in tents made of animal skins or woven grass mats.

From a distance, Mandan earth lodges looked like grass-covered hills. The doorways faced the center of the town, where rituals took place.

THE PLAINS

Hundreds of years ago, farming people lived in earth lodges along the rivers in the eastern part of the Great Plains. An earth lodge was built by setting four posts upright in the bottom of a pit dug in the ground. The posts held up the roof. The lodge was then covered with layers of poles, grass, and dirt.

Few people lived on the western Great Plains all year long until the Native Americans got horses. Europeans brought horses to the Americas in the 1500s. By the 1700s, the animals had reached the Plains tribes.

The ancestors of the Cheyenne, Lakota, and Arikara had been farmers who lived east of the Great Plains. But when they got horses, they gave up earth lodges and farming to live on the western Plains.

The great herds of buffalo provided these tribes with food and clothing. They lived in tipis—buffalo-skin tents that were made by the women.

With horses, Native Americans were able to

People had always hunted buffalo on the Plains. But after the Native Americans got horses from the Europeans, these hunts became more daring.

move around more and meet many other tribes. These tribes had different languages, so the Native Americans invented a sign language. They used hand gestures to talk with each other.

THE PLATEAU REGION

The tribes of the Plateau region west of the Rocky Mountains lived in pit houses during the winter. During the summer they lived in tents.

This Plateau pit house has the top covering removed to show the inside ladder, the four roof supports, and the side poles that hold up the ceiling.

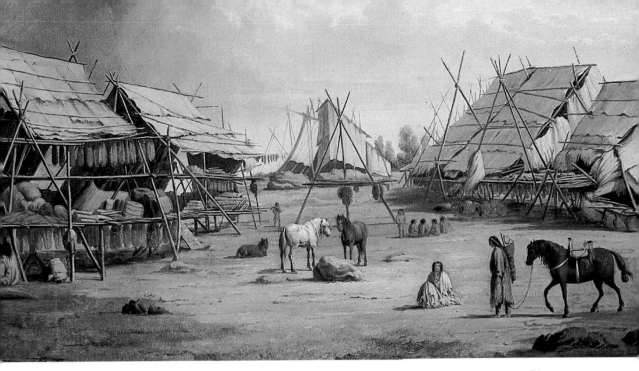

Fishing was an important part of life on the Plateau. In this painting salmon are hanging from poles to dry, and stored in soft bags.

Pit houses were dug deep into the earth and covered over with a sturdy roof. A ladder leading to a door in the roof allowed people to come and go. These tribes fished for salmon and gathered tasty roots.

In California, acorns were an important food. They were stored in baskets until they could be ground and processed into flour.

CALIFORNIA

Earth lodges were used by tribes in parts of California. Flour was made from acorns— after poisonous acids were removed by washing.

These tribes had fewer links with other tribes. California has many mountains and valleys, and travel was difficult.

Huge houses like this one were built on the Northwest Coast. The homes of important leaders had faces painted and carved on the front. Wooden totem poles stood nearby.

THE NORTHWEST COAST

In the Northwest, cedar trees were cut down and split into planks to make huge houses. As many as fifty people lived in one house.

The people ate many kinds of salmon, berries,

A totem pole (left) with a thunderbird on the top and a bear on the bottom. Masks (top right) were used by Tlingit doctors when they cured people. When Native Americans became Christians, they had to get rid of these objects. Beautiful baskets (above) were made by women of the Northwest Coast tribes.

and meat. During the winter, they feasted on stored foods. They spent **40** much of their time in rituals. They wore sacred masks when they danced.

During a festival called a potlatch, leaders gave away food and gifts to show that they were kind and helpful.

The cedar tree provided many of the people's needs. Its wood was carved into houses, boxes, and canoes. Its bark was shredded and woven into clothing. Its roots were made into baskets.

Boxes were used for storage and for cooking. How did they cook in a wooden box? First, rocks were heated in a fire. Then, one at a time, the hot rocks were dropped into a box full of water. Soon, the water boiled and the food was cooked.

Native children were taken away from their families and sent to boarding schools like this one. They were taught to be like white people and to be ashamed of their traditions. This was wrong.

CHANGES

After the Europeans came, native peoples all over America changed the way they lived. Sometimes they changed because they liked the new ways better. But, more often, change was forced upon them.

Native Americans were told that their languages were too hard to speak and their religions were false. This made them sad. They began to lose pride in themselves and their ways of life. Times were hard for them.

Today, most Native Americans live in ordinary houses and buy their food from grocery stores. They travel in trucks and cars.

But sometimes, especially during times of worship, a family stays in a house like

Every summer, native people wear tribal clothes and attend powwows and other gatherings where they can enjoy being the first Americans. Drumming, singing, and dancing still play an important part in native life.

the one their ancestors lived in. They eat the foods that nature has always provided for them. They celebrate their ancient traditions. They live again in harmony with the land and the waters.

45

WORDS YOU SHOULD KNOW

acorn (A • korn) — the brown, nutlike seed of an oak tree

adobe (uh • DOH • bee) — bricks made of sand, clay, and straw

ancestors (AN • sess • terz) — grandparents, or forebears who lived long ago

ancient (AIN • shint) — very old

buffalo (BUFF • ah • low) — a large hoofed animal with short horns and a humped back; also called a bison

canoe (kuh • NOO) — a small boat made from a hollowed-out log or from a wooden frame covered with sheets of bark

ceremony (SAIR • ih • moh • nee) — a celebration or a religious service

copper (KAH • per) — a soft and shiny reddish metal

culture (KUL • cher) — ideas, actions, and habits that children learn as they grow up in a certain group of people

customs (KUSS • tumz) — usual ways of doing things

descendant (dih • SEN • dint) — a child or a grandchild; a person who comes later in a family line

environment (en • VYE • run • mint) — the natural things that surround us; the lands and waters of the earth

explorer (ex • PLOR • er) — a person who travels to new places to learn about the land and the people there

fasting (FAST • ing) — going without food

harmony (HAR • muh • nee) — unity; cooperation

invent (in • VENT) — to create or develop

mica (MIKE • uh) — a shiny mineral that forms thin layers, used for decoration

native (NAY • tiv) — a person who belongs to a certain place

nourishing (NER • ih • shing) — giving health and strength

obsidian (ahb • SID • ee • yan) — a glassy, black rock that holds an edge when used for knife blades or arrow points

potlatch (PAHT • latch) — a ceremony of the Northwest peoples in which a person gives away valuable presents and food

reeds (REEDZ) — water plants that have strong, stiff stems

refugees (REH • fyoo • jeez) — people who leave their homeland because of conditions there, such as war or famine

ritual (RIT • choo • il) — a special set of actions used in religious ceremonies

tipi (TEE • pee) — a movable tent made of long pine poles set in a cone shape and covered with animal skins

INDEX

About the Author

Jay Miller lives in Seattle so he can eat salmon and visit the nearby reservations, mountains, streams, and ocean. He enjoys hiking in the mountains, kayaking, and eating pie as much as he enjoys being a writer, professor, and lecturer. His family is complex but delightful. He is proud to be a member of the Delaware Wolf clan.

He went to college at the University of New Mexico and Rutgers University. He also learned from elders all over the Americas, who taught him the best stuff of all.

For help in writing this book, he wants to thank Vi, Noah, Zachary, and Sara. Rebecca, Keri, Megan, Garrett, Erica, and Aaron also helped in their own ways.